Studies and Melodious Etudes for French Horn

by

James Ployhar

To The Teacher

"Studies And Melodious Etudes", Level II, is a supplementary technic book of the Belwin "STUDENT INSTRUMENTAL COURSE". Although planned as a companion and correlating book to the method, "The French Horn Student", it can also be used effectively with most intermediate French Horn instruction books. It provides for extended and additional treatment in technical areas, which are limited in the basic method because of lack of space. Emphasis is on developing musicianship through scales, warm-ups and technical drills, musicianship studies and interesting melody-like etudes.

The Belwin "STUDENT INSTRUMENTAL COURSE" - A course for individual and class instruction of LIKE instruments, at three levels, for all band instruments.

EACH BOOK IS COMPLETE IN ITSELF BUT ALL BOOKS ARE CORRELATED WITH EACH OTHER

METHOD
"The French Horn Student"
For individual
or
class instruction.
(cannot be used with other brass instruments.)

ALTHOUGH EACH BOOK CAN BE USED SEPARATELY, IDEALLY, ALL SUPPLEMENTARY BOOKS SHOULD BE USED AS COMPANION BOOKS WITH THE METHOD

STUDIES AND MELODIOUS ETUDES

Supplementary scales, warm-up and technical drills, musicianship studies and melody-like etudes all carefully correlated with the method.

TUNES FOR TECHNIC

Technical type melodies, variations, and "famous passages" from musical literature — for the development of technical dexterity.

FRENCH HORN SOLOS

Four separate correlated solos, with piano accompaniment, written or arranged by James D. Ployhar:

Sonata Theme .... *W. A. Mozart*
Themes from "Academic Festival Overture"............. *J. Brahms*
The Hunt.........*James D. Ployhar*
Caprice............*James D. Ployhar*

BIC 00252

Fingering Chart for the Double French Horn (F&B♭)

Since the Double Horn is now in common use the following chart contains fingerings for both the F Horn and the B♭ Horn. The use of the B♭ Horn allows for greater accuracy in the high register and facilitates tone production in the low register. Not all tones are practical on the B♭ Horn, however, because of intonation problems.

Many players prefer to use their B♭ Horn when they reach second line G♯ and continue to use it throughout the upper register.

The B♭ Horn is also employed from low F down to low C.

If you have a Double Horn your teacher will advise you when to use it. When playing lip slurring exercises in this book the fingerings indicated are for F Horn.

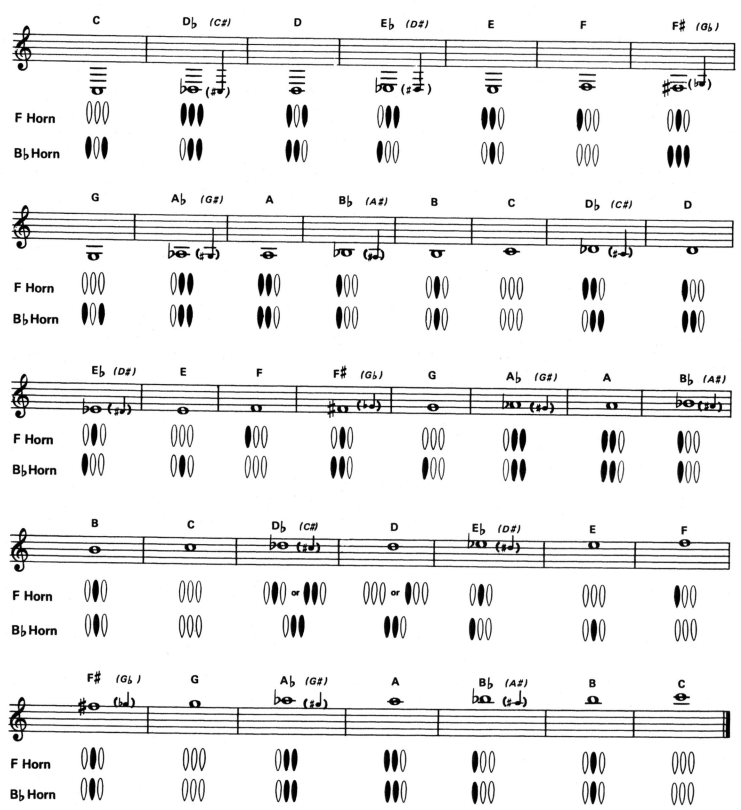

The Studies and Etudes on this page correlate approximately with Page 5, Lesson 2 of the French Horn Method Book THE FRENCH HORN STUDENT, Level II, and the correlation is continued throughout the book.

Slowly

1st + 2nd valves _____   2nd + 3rd valves _____   1st + 2nd valves _____

a minor Scale (Harmonic form)

Also play: etc.

Etude No. 1

Moderato

mf

4

Etude No. 2

A BAR across the stem means divide the note into eighth notes.

F HORN

Slowly

f

1st valve_____

1st + 2nd valves_____   2nd + 3rd valves _____   1st + 2nd valves _____
3rd

d minor scale (Melodic form)

Practice slowly, and then try for speed.

Also play: etc.

Etude No. 3

2/2

Moderato

mp

a tempo

rit.

Etude No. 4

Etude No. 5

Work for speed!

Also play:

Practice slowly with crisp, clean tonguing. Then work for speed.

Etude No. 6

1st + 2nd valves_____ 2nd + 3rd valves_____ 1st + 3rd valves_____

Count: 1 + 2 +

Count: 1 + 2 +

Etude No. 7

Moderato

mf

1st + 2nd valves _____ 2nd + 3rd valves _____ 1st + 3rd valves _____

Practice slowy, and then try for speed.

Etude No. 8

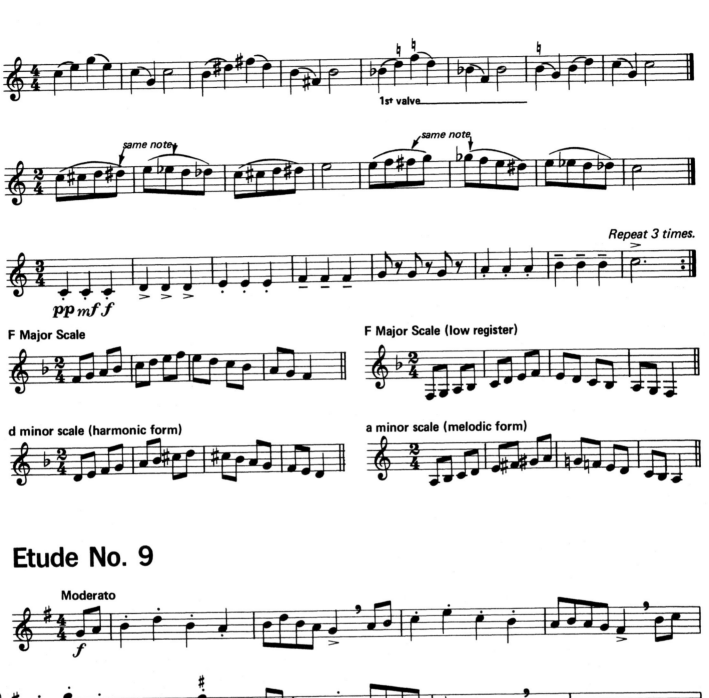

Etude No. 9

1st + 2nd valves _____ 2nd + 3rd valves _____ 1st + 3rd valves _____

Apply these rhythms to the scale above:

① ② ③ ④ ⑤

G Major Scale

Bb Major Scale

e minor scale (melodic form)

G Major Scale (low register)

Etude No. 10

Allegro

ff

rit.

a tempo

rit.

First, practice with one sharp in Key Signature — then with two flats. (G major and g minor)

Etude No. 11

14

g minor scale (harmonic form)

e minor scale

Apply these rhythms to the scale above:

Etude No. 12

Practice slowy and then try for speed!

1st + 2nd valves _____ 2nd + 3rd valves _____ 1st + 3rd valves _____

Play in a short, detached style.

Also play: etc.

Practice as Slow and Fast ⁶⁄₈

Count-slow 123 4 5 6 1 2 3 4 5 6 1 2 3 4 5 6 etc.
Count-fast 1   2   1   2   1   2   etc.

Practice first with NO flats in Key Signature —— then with three flats. (C Major and c minor)

Etude No. 13

Fast ⁶⁄₈

Count: *f* 1   2

Etude No. 14

1st + 2nd valves ____ 2nd + 3rd valves ____ 1st + 3 rdvalves ____

Also play:

etc.

First play with two sharps in Key signature — then with one flat. (D Major and d minor)

Etude No. 15

ARBAN

Moderato

Slowly (Use standard fingering)

Work for speed.

Also play:

Fast

Count: 1   2

Count: 1   2

Etude No. 16

Majestically

First tongue every note — then play as slurred!

$\frac{1}{4}$ of beat

$\frac{1}{3}$ of beat

Etude No. 17

Moderato

ARBAN

mf

simile

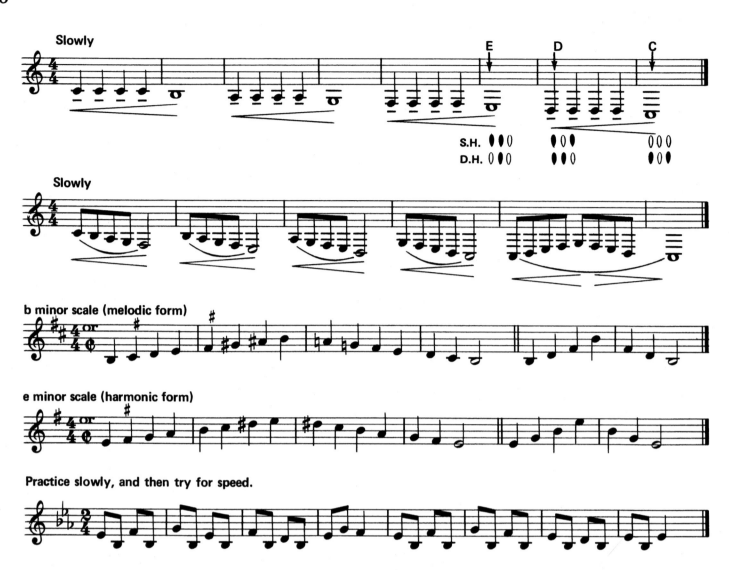

Practice slowly, and then try for speed.

Etude No. 18

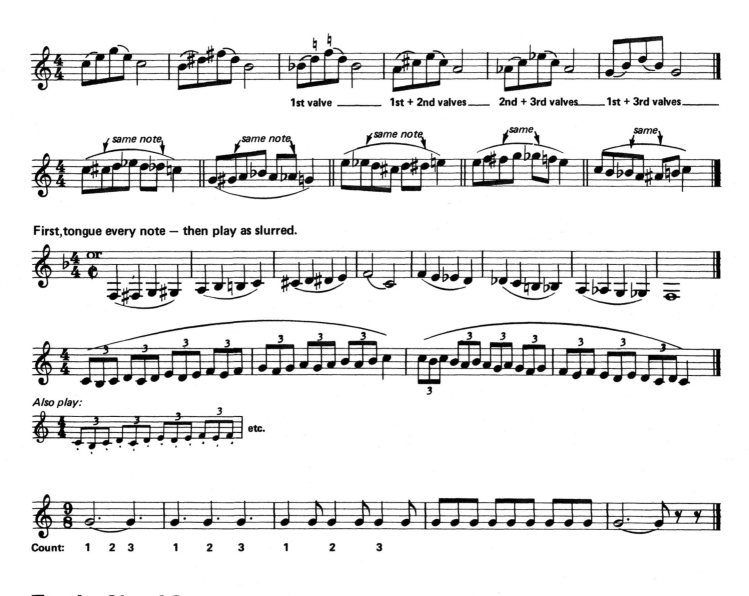

1st valve _____ 1st + 2nd valves _____ 2nd + 3rd valves _____ 1st + 3rd valves _____

First, tongue every note — then play as slurred.

Also play:

Count: 1 2 3   1 2 3   1 2 3

Etude No. 19

Andante con moto

Count: 1   2   3   1   2   3

rit.

1st + 2nd valves____ 2nd + 3rd valves____ 1st + 3rd valves____

Play both ways. Work for speed!

Count carefully!

Work for speed!

Also play:

etc.

Etude No. 20

Moderato

1st + 2nd valves _____

2nd + 3rd valves _____

1st + 3rd valves _____

Play both ways.

Also play: etc.

Etude No. 21

Allegro

CONCONE

mf

Play both ways.

Work for speed!

c minor scale (harmonic form)

Etude No. 22

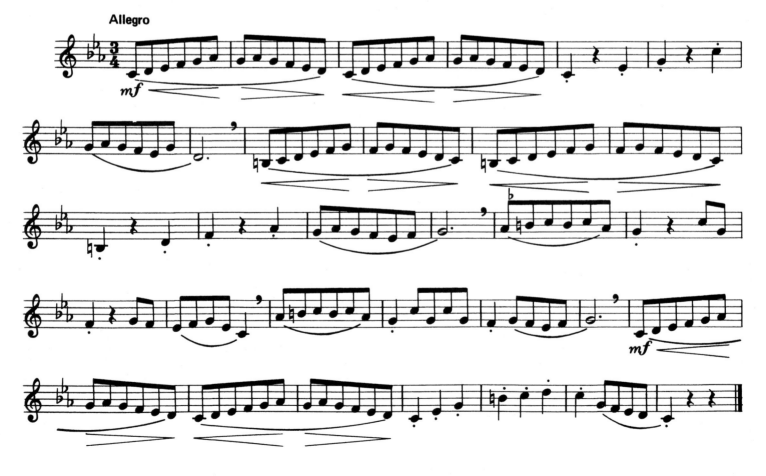

Practice slowly, and then try for speed!

Fast

Eb Major

Also play: etc.

c minor (melodic form)

Also play: etc.

Play entire line with 1st valve

Etude No. 23

Moderato

1st + 2nd valves ———————————— 2nd + 3rd valves———————— 1st + 3rd valves————————

Play in both $\frac{4}{4}$ and $\mathbf{C}$.

* *see note below*

* *see note below*

Etude No. 24

$\downarrow$ divide into two eighth notes. $\ddagger$ divide into four sixteenth notes. $\downarrow$ divide into four eighth notes.

$\downarrow$ divide into triplets.

Play in both **4/4** and **¢**.

A Major Scale

Etude No. 25

1st + 2nd valves _____   2nd + 3rd valves_____   1st + 3rd valves _____

Play in both 𝄴 and ¢

f minor scale (melodic form)   *Like F♮*

Practice slowly, and then try for speed.

Also play: etc.

Etude No. 26

Allegro

Like F♮

Etude No. 27

1st valve_____

1st † 2nd valves_____   2nd + 3rd valves_____   1st + 3rd valves_____

Apply to above scale: Practice slowly, then try for speed:
① ② ③

Also play:
etc.

Etude No. 28

ARBAN

Allegretto

A Major Scale

Etude No. 29

Summary of Commonly Used Major Scales and their Related Minors